GLOSSORY OF THE ONLINE BUSINESS

The Key to the Quick Mastery of
Online Business Terms, Requirements and
Practices

Compiled and Edited

By

Sa'idu Sulaiman

Email: saisulaiman@yahoo.com

ISBN: 9798657353099

Published in 2020

by

Amazon KDP, USA

Excerpts from Author's Previous Works with Glossaries

....

Matching principle: ensuring that expenses incurred in a period are matched against the revenue realized as result of these expenses.

Prepayments: expenses incurred in advance of enjoying their benefits or exhausting the benefits at the end of an accounting period.

Work-in-process: partly finished goods passing through the manufacturing process (also called work-in-process).

From: <u>Understanding Book-keeping and Accounts</u>

....

Globoeconomics: the study of macro-economic variables and policies of a nation, region or the entire globe as they influence or are influenced by macroeconomic variables and polices of other nations or regions due to globalization.

Positive globalism: this means showing love and concern for humanity in general and taking legitimate measures to promote its wellbeing without discriminations based on race, culture and geographical location.

From: <u>12 Facts about Protectionism and the Global Economy</u>

TABLE OF CONTENTS

Contents   Page
Preface   i
About the Author   ii

Entries with numbers   1
Entries for A   3
Entries for B   9
Entries for C   18
Entries for D   34
Entries for E   39
Entries for F   46
Entries for G   49
Entries for H   51
Entries for I   54
Entries for J   57
Entries for K   58
Entries for L   64
Entries for M   69
Entries for N   74
Entries for O   77
Entries for P   81
Entries for Q   86
Entries for R   88
Entries for S   92
Entries for T   100
Entries for U   103
Entries for V   107

Entries for W 109
Entries for X 113
Entries for Y 114
Entries for Z 115

PREFACE

When you master the terminologies used in describing or reporting the process of, and the requirements for operating online businesses, buying their products or services, and working with them, you have already done 70 percent of the task of learning how online businesses operate and flourish.

One way you can follow to master terminologies related to the online business is by taking time to search for them from various sources such as online dictionaries, webpages and weblogs. The quickest way is to use a rich and one stop solution to the problem of searching for the terminologies from scattered sources. This is exactly what this book provides to you.

The benefits of reading this book apply to owners, employees and customers of online businesses as well as third parties that facilitate eCommerce like banks and providers of payment gateways. Knowing the meaning of the terms 'sales funnel' and 'conversion' will, for instance, enable the owner of an online business to understand them when they appear in blog posts and other writings, and also utilize them to boost the business. Another example is that knowing term 'clickbait' will make customers of online businesses wiser when it comes to taking decision on buying products or subscribing to services offered by the businesses.

Lastly, students of Economics, Business Studies and Commerce will find this book useful in this digital era.

About the Author

Sa'idu Sulaiman is a writer, resource person, consultant and a retired Economics Lecturer. He obtained a combined honours degree in Education/Economics in 1985, a Postgraduate Diploma in Management in 1991 and a Master of Business Administration (MBA) in 1997. In 2015, he became a member of the London based Institute for Small Business and Entrepreneurship (ISBE) after attending its 2014 international conference in Manchester, UK.

Mentoring has been is still part of his life. He loves changing people's lives through teaching, writing and mentoring. Consequently, he is the founder of www.obmentors.com which aims to mentor people on online business. Some of his published works include:

9 Requirements for Quality Research and Academic Papers

12 Facts about Protectionism and the Global Economy

The Desperate Migrant

What Matters Most

301 Redirect

This is an instruction given to a web browser to take visitors and search engines that are familiar with your old web address to a new address. If, for instance, your old web address is www.regime.com and the new address is www.myregime.com visitors to the old site will be taken to the new one. The status code of 301 means that the page has been permanently moved to a new location.

302 Redirect

Unlike the 301 redirect which is for a permanent change in your web address, the 302 redirect is used for temporary change in your web address. This redirect is used when your original web page is undergoing repairs or modifications to contents or when you want visitors to see a different page for a limited time.

404 Error

This is a message displayed on a web page when you click on a link or enter a web address that is no longer working, or when you typed the web address incorrectly. The message means that a page cannot be found.

Acquirer/Acquiring Bank

This is a financial institution that processes a payment transaction, such as credit or debit card payments, on behalf of a merchant. The acquirer enables businesses to accept credit card payments for the purchase of goods and services, underwrites the merchant account, and provides the hardware and software to enable the merchant to process transactions.

Address Verification Service (AVS):

This is a process which credit card companies use in their systems to verify whether the billing address of the credit card provided by the user matches the address provided on the credit card statement or in their records.

Ads

This a short way of writing "advertisements"

Adsense

This is an advertising system run by Google. It is available to website owners interested in monetizing their websites by allowing Google to post advertisements in form of text, image, or videos on designated parts of the websites.

Ad Servers

These are servers which store advertisements and serve them to web pages. They facilitate advertisement trafficking and provide reports on advertisement performance.

Advertising Network

An advertising network is a group of websites on which advertisements are purchased through a single sales entity. It could be a collection of sites owned by one publisher or an affiliation of sites sharing a representative. Advertising networks serve as intermediaries between advertisers and publishers. They provide a centralized ad server that can serve advertisements to a number of websites and perform tracking, reporting and targeting functions.

Adwords

This is an advertising platform developed by Google for people interested in promoting their products or services on Google's search engine results page (SERP), Google's Display Network (GDN) and affiliate sites. The text ad that appears as a "sponsored link" among the links that appear in the result page for a query you type in the Google search box, is an example of a search ad.

Affiliate

An affiliate is a website owner who promotes the products or services of another person or business for a commission. As an affiliate, you make money by writing about the product or service you're promoting, and linking this information to the advertiser's page. When visitors to your web page, click on the link, and subsequently, make a purchase, you get a commission from the sale.

Affiliate Marketing

This is a three-party marketing process where a publisher (owner of website) and an advertiser join forces to market products or services to a consumer. The Publisher promotes a service or a specific product by using any form of banners, ads or links to market the product or service to the consumer. The advertiser is the party having the product and is responsible for payment of an agreed upon commission to the publisher from the consequential sales revenue.

Affiliate Networks

These are networks that provide tracking solutions and support to both affiliates and merchants. They provide reporting on programs to both affiliates and merchants, host creative banners, and provide commission payment options. Affiliate networks have many affiliates and merchants that signed up to them. Examples of affiliate networks are Commission Junction, LinkShare and TradeDoubler.

Algorithm

This term commonly refers to Google's Search Algorithm. It is a set of rules Google uses to decide which websites should be included in search results and how they will be ranked.

Analytics

This is the process of collecting and analyzing data about web traffic. The data could be the number of site visitors and the pages that have been visited, etc. Google Analytics is an example of the web analytic software.

Anchor Text

The anchor text is the highlighted or underlined text on a web page. It contains a link to another page within the site or a page on another site.

Application Programming Interface (API)

This term refers to a set of routines, protocols and tools that allows one application to acquire information from another application and uses the information for its own purposes. It's like a common language for applications that allows for conversations. An API gets information from an application and delivers it to you.

Autoresponder

This is an email message which is set to be sent automatically to its recipients. When you sign up for a website, a newsletter or an ebook, for example, you get an email in your inbox within seconds after you clicked "join" or similar call-to- action terms.

Avatar

An avatar is a picture or an icon attached to a person's profile. Avatars also appear beside your name or online alias when you comment on a blog or an online forum.

Average Time on Site

This refers to the amount of time a visitor has spent on a webpage while browsing. It is typically seen in web analytics report and is measured in minutes or seconds.

Backlink

A backlink, also called 'inbound link', is an incoming link to a website coming from a different website. Backlinks are very important in Search Engine Optimization (SEO), they indicate the popularity of a website that has several backlinks.

Blog

The word blog was derived from the combination of the word Web and Log. A blog is an online log of content relevant to your market. It is written in informal conversational style of information or a discussion on specific issues or topics and is updated regularly on a website or a webpage owned by an individual or group of people. Blogs often have images and links to other websites and allow readers to make comments.

Back-End Processor

This terms refers to a data company (often a third party) contracted by an acquirer (or the entity that processes payment transactions on behalf of a merchant) to provide processing and communication services. As opposed to a front-end processor that has connections to the card associations and supplies the acquirer with authorization and settlement services, the back-end processor accepts the settlement information from the front-end processor and routes the payment from the bank that issued the card to the merchant to complete the transaction.

Bank Identification Number (BIN)

This refers to the initial four to six digits that appear on a payment card, identifying the bank or entity that issued the card, the issuer's location, and the card type (credit, debit or gift).

Bank Routing Number

This refers to the first nine digits that appear across the bottom of a personal checque that identifies the financial institution that issued the checque.

Bitcoin

Bitcoin is the most noticeable of an increasing number of decentralized digital currencies, also known as cryptocurrencies, which are not backed by any central bank or government.

Bitcoin

Blockchain

In the field of cryptocurrency transactions, that is, the use of digital currencies exchanged for payments, blockchain is a digital ledger where all transactions, in the form of blocks made in a specific cryptocurrency are recorded in chronological order. The digital ledger is then made publicly available to anyone using that cryptocurrency.

Blogging Ethics

This is the responsibility of bloggers as creators and publishers of knowledge, to be fair, honest, critical in the choice of sources from which materials are lifted, to give credit where it is due and immediately correct mistakes when discovered, and also be respectful towards other content creators but also toward fact. Blogging ethics also entail the responsibility of bloggers to make truthful representation of the topic or issue at hand to ensure its relevance for its readers today and in the distant future, being cautious in the use of clear identifiers of persons in referring to touchy or illegal matters, etc.

Bookmark

A bookmark, also called "favourite" is a marker for web pages and files used to facilitate easy returns to the web pages or files you have left and wished to be visiting again or very often. You bookmark the web page of your favourite online newspaper by simply clicking on the star icon to the right side of its web address or URL box, if you are using the Firefox browser.

Bot

A bot, also known as a 'crawler' or 'spider', refers to software used by search engines, such as Google and Yahoo to explore the Internet for indexing websites. The bot is used to explore website content and capture information taken to search engines for inclusion in their databases.

Bounce Rate

Bounce rate, also called abandonment rate, is the percentage of visitors who enter website and then leave instead of continuing to view other pages within the same site. It is computed by counting the number of single page visits and dividing the total count by the total visits and then expressed as a percentage of total visits. High bounce rates indicate that the website is not good at attracting the continued interest of visitors because visitors only view single pages without looking at others.

Bottom of the Funnel

This is the transaction phase or purchase stage of the online buying process. At this stage, the visitor has done all his/her research and is about to make a purchase, thus becoming a new customer.   This stage is preceded by the 'Top of the Funnel,' that is, the product/service comparison stage and the 'Middle of the Funnel which is the validation stage.

Brick-and-click Store

A brick-and-click store is a business with at least one physical location and an eCommerce-enabled website. It is a business model that captures a customer's attention in both the real and the virtual world. It is an upgrade to the brick-and-mortar business.

Brick and Mortar

This is a business that has a physical store that customers can visit rather than just having an online presence.

Browser

A browser is the software used to view web pages, graphics, and any other online content. Browsers take codes such as HTML, CSS, and Javascript from a website and then translate it into the visually-friendly content you see on the site. Examples of commonly used browsers include Google Chrome, Firefox, Internet Explorer, and Opera.

Bundling

Bundling is a marketing strategy in which several similar products or services are combined together and sold as a bundle or as one package solution, often at a reduced price so as to attract more customers. A seller of stationery, for instance, can offer exercise books, jotters, drawing books, pens and colour pencils as bundle to be purchased at a reduced price.

Business Blogging

This means creating and publishing a corporate blog with a view to achieving company's business goals. It is a marketing method used by companies to communicate better with customers, suppliers, partners, shareholders, employees, etc.

Business-to-Business (B2B)

This is business model which refers to companies selling products or services to other businesses.

Business-to-Consumer (B2C)

This is a business model where companies offer products or services directly to consumers.

Buy-to-Detail Rate

This is a measure that allows you to determine unique purchases per number of views of product details page. It helps you to know the products that users buy after browsing through the product details.

Buy-to-Detail Rate = Total Unique Purchases of a product / Product Detail Page views.

Buyers' Persona

This is a semi-fictional representation of your prospective customer based on market research and actual data of your customers. It reveals buyers' decisions, specific attitudes, concerns, goals, demographics, etc.

Cache

Also called 'browser cache', a catch is a temporary storage location on your computer for files that have been downloaded by your browser in order to display websites and permit web visitors to experience quicker load times. The files include graphic images and other multimedia content.

Call-to-Action (CTA)

This is essentially an invitation to website visitors to make use of an offer, take an action or purchase a good. It appears in the form of a text link, button, or image. Examples of CTAs are "Download the E-guide", "Subscribe Now", or "Buy Now".

Canonical Name (CNAME)

This is also referred to as Canonical Domain. It works as an alias for domains. If, for example, your domain is www.fourhouses1.com, and you point the content of www.fourhouses2.com to it, visitors who enter www.fourhouses1.com, on their web browser's URL box will see the content from www.fourhouses2.com.

Canonical Tag

This term refers to a hidden message on a web page telling search engines that the content on a specific URL is only a duplicate of the content on a different URL. With this tag you can avoid search engine optimization (SEO) issues caused by duplicate content appearing on multiple URLs by "telling" search engines the version of the content that should appear in search results.

Captcha

This is a means preventing spams. It usually comes in the form of a challenge test which is hard for a bot to resolve. Examples of captcha are asking a visitor to a web page to type distorted characters shown on the screen or click on the images that fit a given criteria when signing up for membership.

An example of Capcha

Cart Abandonment Rate

This is the rate at which visitors initiate the purchase by adding an item to their cart and leave the site without completing the transaction. This statistics can be used to assess the success or failure of an online business.

Cascading Style Sheet (CSS)

This refers to the language used by web developers to format the design and layout of a website with a view to making background images, fonts and colours uniform all throughout the site. With this, a single modification made by web developer on the

CSS will be automatically applied to all the web pages.

Case Sensitive

Being case sensitive means being able to distinguish between capital letters (uppercase) and small letters (lowercase). The password you used when signing in on web page are typically case sensitive, you have to type the letters in the exact way you have entered them when creating the password. If your created password is, for example, <u>AZFNMMO145&,</u> you cannot sign in with <u>azfnmmo145&</u> or <u>AZfnmMO145&.</u>

Chargebacks

A chargeback is the reversal of funds to a customer after payment for goods or services. Chargebacks are designed to protect credit/debit cardholders from fraud. Chargebacks are applied when customers feel they have not been given the right product or if the transaction is fraudulent. Frequency of chargebacks indicates problems with the payment solution firm.

Churn

This term refers to customers that have ended their relationship with a business. When a customer signed up for an email newsletter but later unsubscribed, the customer forms part of the business' churn list. A long churn list indicates customers' dissatisfaction with the email newsletter.

Churn Rate

Churn rate, also called attrition rate, is the percentage of customers or subscribers who ended their relationship with a company in the given period of time, usually a month. It is the total number of customers lost during a specific period by unsubscribing from the services offered by a firm.

Clickbait

This refers to any content written in a manner which entices people to click it. Some clickbait techniques are stating unbelievable results (e.g. Take three pills of this medicine and get cured in just 3 days) and telling mysterious stories (e.g. Man Wins the Writing Competition after Reading this Book").

Clickstream

A clickstream refers to the record of everything clicked by people when they browse the web. Every time a visitor clicks on a link, image, or object on a web page, is recorded and stored for learning about the visitors' browsing habits and preferences. Advertisements you often see on the web pages you visit now and in your email box, often reflect your browsing habit gathered from your previous visits to web pages.

Click through Rate (CTR)

This is a means of gauging whether or not an online advertising campaign for a website is successful. The rate is calculated by dividing the number of people who click on a specific link on a website by the total number of people who have viewed the web page or advertisement. CTR helps online retailers to understand the effectiveness of keywords and performances of advertisements and email campaigns. If, for instance, there were 5 clicks on an advertisement and 100 impressions (the number of times this advertisement was shown), then CTR = Clicks/Impressions = 0.05%.

Closed-Loop Marketing

This is an effective method of analytics for achieving better insights into marketing campaigns that could bring good return on investment. The method comprises collection of customer data from multiple channels, analyzing and using it to create appropriate content for targeted customers.

Cohort Analysis

This is an analysis of customer behavior that is divided into groups of people having same attributes to enable marketers to assess long-term trends in customer relation.

Compression

Compression refers to a reduction of the size of an image file so that it can be downloaded or uploaded faster. Since the loading of very large image takes long time, compressing the file size makes it to lose some quality but it will load or show much faster on the web page.

Content Curation

Content curation refers to the process of going through existing content on the web, choosing the best samples and sharing them online. It is a way to adding value to your brand by providing your customers and other online audience with relevant information. If your business, for example, is providing educational services, sharing posts related to these services from a social media page like Facebook is a way of doing content curation.

Content Delivery Network (CDN)

Content delivery network (also called Content Distribution Network) is the network of servers around the globe meant to save website content such as images and videos. With the use of many servers scattered across countries, visitors can load websites faster because of their closeness to the source of the data. Without CDNs, web page visitor from Nigeria or Kenya, for example, would wait for a longer time for the page to load when its server is located in the United States of America.

Content Management System (CMS)

This is a software solution that makes it possible for people to create, update, organize and publish digital content on the Internet with one interface or administration tool. CMS is a tool for people who have no technical expertise to create and manage websites. Examples of CMS systems are WordPress, Drupal, Joomla and SilverStripe.

Content Optimization System (COS)

This is a holistic solution that allows content providers to manage their websites and other constituents of digital marketing all together in one system. It provides them with sales-ready websites that allows easy updates, a personalized look and feel, and provides a variety of techniques for improving search results and rankings.

Content Upgrade

A content upgrade, also called 'lead magnet', is extra content given to people, usually in exchange for their email address. It is something that you give away for free in exchange for a visitor's signing up for your email newsletter or something you get for free in exchange for opting-in to someone's email list. The free content offered could be in the form of a downloadable e-book or access to a special video. It is called content "upgrade" because it is normally an upgrade of what you're already reading from a blog or web page.

Conversion

Conversion refers to your transformation from a visitor to web page selling a product or service to a user or customer signing up for an email newsletter, registration for a free seminar, downloading an online coupon, or making an online purchase.

Conversion Funnel

This term refers to the sequences of events that occur during the customer's journey of buying goods and services online. It begins from initiating a purchase to the navigation process and eventually to converting into a sale. It is called a funnel because at every stage, the number of visitors decreases and at the final stage of purchasing goods or services, the number of buyers is smallest compared to what obtains at the preceding stages of the buying process.

Conversion Path

Conversion path is a series of website based events undertaken by the visitor that might convert into a potential lead. It begins when a visitor first comes to a landing page, browses through series of page transitions and finally reaches the stage of either purchasing a product or service or abandoning it.

Conversion Rate

This is the percentage of people that have completed a desired action on a single web page, such as making an online purchase, signing –up for an e-course or a premium content, etc. Having a high conversion rate means that visitors to the website highly accept what the site offers.

Conversion Rate Optimization (CRO)

This is a process of improving the user experience of your website to increase the chances of convincing its visitors to fully achieve their online goal. The process entails amendments to the web layout, improving content and design based on your understanding of web design basics, human psychology, etc.

Cookies

A cookie is a file stored in your computer by the browser when you visit a website. Cookies allow the websites visited to identify returning visitors and to improve their experiences by resuming where they left off. The main purpose of cookies is to remember information about you and record your preferences when using a particular website. Users often see a pop-up requesting them to accept the cookies. After confirmation, the information in these text files is sent back over to the server.

Copywriting

Copywriting is not copyrighting, it is the act of writing a copy. Copy means a text written to advertise or promote something. All the text on your website constitutes a "copy". You can write it yourself or hire a professional copywriter to write it for you.

Cost Per Action (CPA)

This is a fixed commission paid to an affiliate marketer for a particular action.

Cost-Per-Click (CPC)

This is a pricing model for advertising campaigns by which an advertiser pays a certain amount of money to a search engine for each user's click on a link in an online advertisement that takes him/her to the advertiser's website.

Cost Per Lead

This is a pricing model for advertising campaigns. It is used by marketers to generate a newsletter list, rewards programme, etc., by connecting with people who are interested in the marketers' brands. In this model the advertiser is charged only when site visitors fully fill out the sign-up form.

Cost Per Sale [CPS])

This is also called revenue share. It is an agreed-on percentage of the purchase amount paid to an affiliate marketer.

Cost-Per-Thousand (CPM)

This is a pricing model for advertising campaigns in which advertisers pay a certain amount of money for every 1,000 visitors to web pages who see their advertisements, even if the visitors do not click on the advertisements or make a purchase.

Crawler

A crawler is also called a 'bot' or 'spider'. It refers to software used by search engines to explore the Internet to locate and index websites and also capture information for storage in search engines' databases.

Cross-Selling

This is the selling of additional services or products to the customers that already made a purchase. It is employed to inspire existing customers to buy products that are complementary or related to what they have already purchased. An example for cross-selling used by online retailers is the statement 'Customers who bought this item also bought...'

Crowdsourcing

This is a practice of an intelligent gathering of information from a group of people to achieve a business goal. This involves getting content, ideas and opinions from a large group of people through the Internet and social media apps. People taking part in crowdsourcing can work as paid freelancers, while others perform small tasks on a voluntary basis. Examples of firms that use crowdsourcing campaigns are Doritos and Airbnb.

Customer Relationship Management (CRM)

This is a means of compiling, managing and analyzing information on customer's interactions with your business throughout the customer life-cycle to improve customer relationship and, subsequently, achieve business goals. CRM also refers to software that businesses use to track, manage, and analyze data about their customers and potential customers with a view to generating revenue by improving their interactions with contacts. The information that is usually compiled with the CRM software includes customer contacts, purchases, customer service and technical support provided, etc., it comes from different channels, such as company's website, telephone, live chat, direct mail, and social media. Examples of CRM software include Marketing 360, Pipedrive and Really Simple Systems.

Customer Acquisition Cost (CAC)

This is the cost of convincing a customer to buy a product or service. It is a business metrics associated with the cost of acquiring and convincing potential customers. It includes expenses related to product cost, research, marketing and incentives. For instance, if a business owner spends $2000 on marketing in a given year and is able to acquire 200 customers in that year, the CAC would be $10.00 (i.e $2000/200). CAC is helpful when you want to determine how to allocate resources while gaining new customers.

Customer Lifetime Value (CLV)

This is also called Lifetime Customer Value (LCV) or Lifetime value (LTV). It is an estimate of the total value (total net profit) an online business company would make from the lifetime relationship it would have with any given customer.

Digital Commerce

This refers to the entire eCommerce system comprising analytics from search engines, social platforms, mobile apps, and other angles of the Internet and the world of commerce.

Discount Code

This also called as a Coupon code or Promo code. It is a code that consists of computer-generated letters and numbers used to activate discounts or special offers made on a website. The code is made available via email or advertisements and entered in the promotional box on the website, shopping cart and the checkout page. A retailer, can, for instance, send promotional email to a given customer offering him/her a 15% discount on using a discount code (for instance, WMR244D) while making a purchase on his site. The customer will enter the code on the cart page before making the payment to get the 15% discount on the whole order. This serves as a marketing strategy to attract more traffic on the site.

Discount Rate

This is a percentage of each purchase charged by acquiring banks for processing a merchant's transactions. It is usually a small percentage of each purchase and it depends on several factors like type of payment card and how credit card is processed and order placed, etc.

Distributed Denial of Service (DDoS)

This is the condition of going offline which a website experiences when flooded with so much fake traffic in the form of fake visits by non-human beings.

Direct Traffic

Direct traffic is one of the most common sources of visits to your website. It comprises visitors who manually type your website's URL into their browser or clicked on a bookmark. When a visitor follows a link from one website to another, the site of origin is the referrer. Referrer sites include search engines, social media, blogs, or other websites providing you with links to other websites.

DoFollow Link

In Search Engine Optimization (SEO), a dofollow link tells search engines to follow a link and reach the website where it leads. If, for instance, the phrase "click here" is linked to the web page www.onlineshop2.com/pricelist, when you click on the phrase it will lead you to that web page and search engines will also see the page and add it to their Search Engine Results Page (SERP).

Domain

This term refers to a user-friendly name used as an address for your website. It can be composed by using any combination of letters and numbers, like obmentors.com, hobbies200.com, or ayyamuleid.com. Each website has a unique domain so when you register it, it will lead people to only your website.

Domain Name Service (DNS)

This is also called domain name system. It is an Internet service that translates domain names into Internet Protocol (IP) addresses. It is like a phonebook for websites having domain names instead of people's names, and IP addresses, instead of phone numbers. A DNS is easier for people to remember but computers use IP addresses to access websites. A DNS is needed to translate your domain name into an IP address.

Downsell

This is a sales strategy for selling a more affordable product to customers after they reject your main product. For example, if your customers refuse to buy a 200-page printed book at $30, you divide it into two volumes and sell each at $14.

Dropshipping

This is a type of eCommerce in which you make an arrangement or agreement with a manufacturer or wholesaler of products to ship them directly to your customers. This means you don't hold stock but pay a greater cost per item sold. The dropshipping business can be done in two ways: merchants can make an arrangement to purchase goods as needed by their customers for manufacturers or wholesalers to fulfill order requirements; or merchants who partner with suppliers or manufacturers can give the shipping addresses of their customers so that products can shipped directly to the customers upon request.

Duplicate Content

This means two or more URLs showing the same content. When this happens, a problem in Search Engine Optimization (SEO) is created because search engines will find it difficult to determine which duplicate is the most relevant.

eBay

This is very popular eCommerce site that provides an online auction service. It uses an electronic platform to allow consumers and businesses to buy and sell wide range of goods and services worldwide.

eBook

An eBook (also called electronic book) is a digital version of a printed book which can be read on a computer, mobile phone and e-reader devices. An eBook consists of text and images and can be published in different file formats like plain text, PDF, Rich Text Format, image files and Epub.

eCommerce

This is the process of buying and selling goods and services online or electronically. This term may refer to online retail as a whole, or more specifically the transaction type.

E-course

This is on online course designed to contain course objectives and learning material as well as interactive sessions between the trainer and trainees through e-mails, phone calls, videos and real time online coaching. While e-books are easier to produce than e-courses and cost less, e-courses demand a lot from course organizers, that's why they charge you more for them.

Editorial Calendar

The editorial calendar is a means of scheduling and controlling the publication of content and keeping track of what to write next and when. With this calendar, publishers and bloggers can easily control publishing of content on different medium or platform like print, online, video, etc.

E-guide

An e-guide is a digital version of a guide that is usually loaded with expected learning outcomes, learning material, exercises, works sheets and steps to be followed to accomplish certain tasks. Examples of such tasks can be establishing an online journal, turning a conventional shopping mall into an online store, etc.

Electronic Bill Payment

Electronic bill payment is a method of sending money to a seller's or creditor's bank account directly from an existing bank account. This method can also be used to pay credit card or other bills.

Electronic Check

The electronic check also called ACH or eCheck, is a method of payment which draws cash from a checking account, eliminating the use of paper check and the inconvenience of sending it physically.

Email

Email is short for 'electronic mail' and is a method of exchanging digital messages to specified recipients using digital devices such as computers, tablets and mobile phones. Emails can contain text, files, images and attachments.

Email Client

An Email client is what you use to read, send, and receive emails. Gmail, Yahoo and Outlook are examples of email clients.

Email Service Provider (ESP)

This is a company that offers email marketing or bulk email services, making it easy for marketers and entrepreneurs to create email marketing campaigns and send them to their distribution lists. Examples of companies that serve as ESPs include Convertkit, Active Campaign and Mailchimp.

Email Sequence

This term refers to a series of emails set up to automatically send out to your email subscribers. 2 to 5 emails, for instance, can be set up to automatically be sent out to anyone that signs up to your email list to introduce him or her to your products or services.

Email Traffic

This is the number of visits made to your website from people who have received emails from, and have clicked the link leading to your web page. The amount of email traffic received by a website can be used to determine the effectiveness of your email marketing campaigns in attracting visitors to it.

Embed

To embed means to add content from another site like YouTube videos into your own web or blog pages.

Emoji

This is a small image used to express an emotion, such as a smiley or a heart used a substitute for body language in text messages, personal emails, social media posts, etc.

An emoji for a smiling face

Engagement

This refers to ways people react or interact with a piece of content. It can be measured in the form of clicks, likes, shares, etc.

Engagement Rate

Engagement Rate is a metric that is used to measure how much a visitor gets engaged to the given piece of content or advertisement. It shows a percentage of the people who came to your site and became engaged with it. Users' comments, likes and their shares help you to determine their interest and willingness to know more about displayed content or advertisement. The formula for calculating the engagement rate is *the total number of reactions, comments and shares for a particular period* divided by *the total reach derived for the posts for the same period* multiplied by *100.*

Event-Triggered Email

An event-triggered-email is an automated email message sent to the list of subscribers when a particular event occurs with the help of the information they have entered while registering on your website. For instance, a special message is sent to subscribers on their respective birthdays which they provided at the time of registering. Triggered based emails are marketing tools that make your customers feel valued and remain with your business.

Evergreen Content

This is a content which remains relevant and valuable to the readers a long time after its publication, so it provides revenue to its creator for a long period. Examples of evergreen content include how-to guides, personal stories, a list of resources, etc.

External Link

This is a link that is put on a web page to direct readers to a web page on a different website.

Ezine

An electronic magazine, whether delivered via a web site or an email.

File Transfer Protocol (FTP)

This is a means of transferring files between computers on a network. With a FTP client, you can review the files from a website and see them in a similar way as the files on your computer and even save them to your computer.

Floating Advertisement

This is an advertisement that appears in a layer over the content of a website, not in a separate window. Usually, the user can close it.

Following

Following, also called "social following", is the group of people who have chosen to receive updates from you on your social media pages.

Follower

A follower is visitor to your page who chooses to see updates from you on a social media sites, like Facebook or Instagram.

Frequently Asked Questions (FAQs)

This is a section of a website where a visitor can view common questions, asked by other customers or visitors, about the products or services offered.

Fulfillment

Fulfillment also called or Order Fulfillment, refers to a sequence of steps a company follows to process the order from the point of sale to the delivery of goods with customer satisfaction. It is third-party service which looks after warehousing, stock management and delivery.

Funnel

In online business, funnel refers to the different stages of a website visitors' journey before they finally decide to buy a product or service. The journey is called a funnel because at the beginning of the journey there are many visitors but as they move through the next stages, some of them drop out. At the stage of making a purchase, only a few visitors remain.

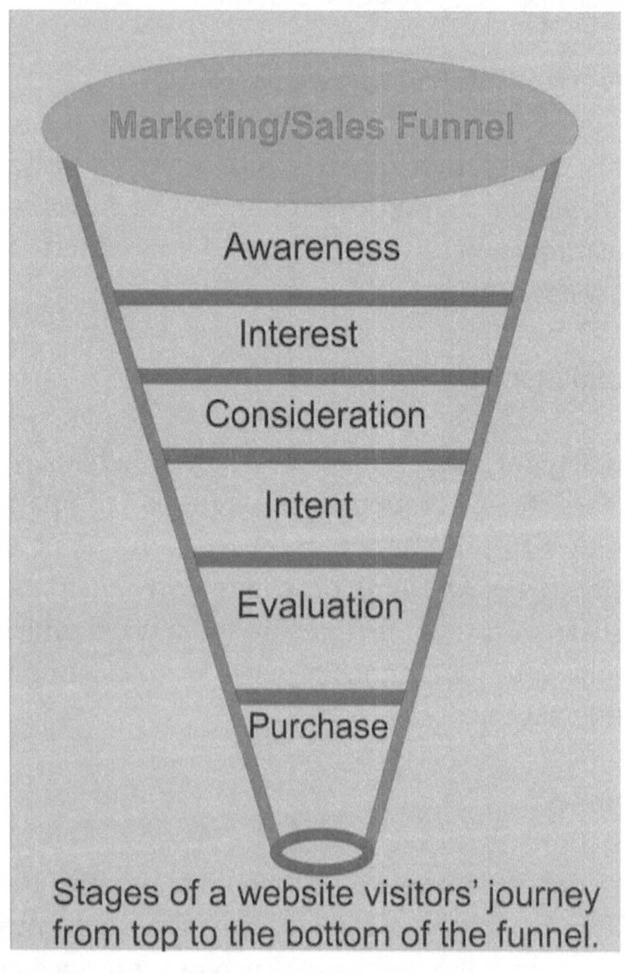

Stages of a sales funnel

GIF

Graphics Interchange Format (GIF), unlike other file formats like JPG, JPEG, and PNG, can be a static image that does not move or an animated image (moving image like a video clip). GIFs are usually seen on social media when short clips from movies are shared without audio.

Gift Cards

A gift card is a prepaid stored-value card, issued by a bank or retail business. It is meant to serve as an alternative to cash for the purchase of goods or services. Its monetary value is stored on the card itself and not in an external account owned by a merchant or a financial institution.

Gig Economy

This is a labour supply system dominated by independent contractors and freelancers instead of the traditional full-time employees. The contractor or freelancer is paid for each "gig" or short-term job performed. The Gig economy is a term increasingly used in reference to the rise of on-demand services provided by businesses like DoorDash and Uber.

Google Analytics

Google Analytics is a free tool you can link up with your website to track traffic through your site and their interactions with your goals. It provides invaluable insights about your website.

Hacker

The term "hacker" refers to a cybercriminal, often an expert programmer, who gains unauthorized access to systems, networks and data to commit crimes.

Hashtag

This a label or a phrase preceded by a hash character (#) used in social networks and microblogging services to identify the messages of specific topics. When you use them, you are helping people who are interested in your topic discover your posts, so it is principally useful for promotions. If your business is, for example, selling car accessories, you can use #newcaraccessories and #getyourcaraccessories on your social network pages for your followers to view other posts related to these topics by just clicking on these hashtags.

Header Image

Header image is the primary, full-width image that appears at the top of a web page, social media account or an email message.

Hero Image

This is a large banner image frequently spread across the width of a web page. It is often the first graphic image you see when you visit a website.

Homepage

A homepage is the first web page viewed when you enter the domain of website in the URL field of your web browser. For instance, if you open Firefox or Google Chrome and type in obmentors.com, the first page that appears is the home page of this website.

Hyperlink

A hyperlink, or simply 'link', is what connects an element that appears web page (e.g. a text, button, or image) to another part of the page or another web page. When the link directs a user to a page on a different website, it is called an external link.

Hypertext Markup Language (HTML)

This is the language used to create websites. Its markups are incorporated in the content of a web page which can then be seen by users in web browsers.

Hypertext Transfer Protocol (HTTP)

Hypertext Transfer Protocol is the standard network protocol that web browsers and servers use to communicate over the web. It is put before the "www" of a URL. E.g. (http://www.obmentors.com).

Hypertext Transfer Protocol Secured (HTTPS)

Hypertext Transfer Protocol Secured is similar to HTTP, adding the suffix 'secured' means that the communication includes a special layer of encryption to protect sensitive information. For example, https://www.obmentors.com is more secure than http://www.obmentors.com

ICANN

The Internet Corporation for Assigned Names and Numbers (ICANN) is the body responsible for coordinating the management of the technical elements of the DNS to ensure universal resolvability so that all users of the Internet can find all valid addresses. This is achieved by overseeing the distribution of unique technical identifiers used in the Internet's operations, and delegation of Top-Level Domain names (TLDs) such as .com, .info, .biz, .ng, .uk, etc.

Impressions

This is an advertising term which means the number of times an advertisement was seen by its target audience.

Inbound Link

An inbound link, also called a 'backlink', is an incoming link to a website coming from another website. This type of link is useful in search engine optimization. Having many inbound links in your website indicates its popularity.

Influencer

An influencer is a person with great influence over other people's opinions. Examples of influencers include celebrities like film actors and football players, industry experts, popular lecturers, preachers and inspirational speakers. They can influence people to buy and use certain products and services thereby increasing sales.

Internet Protocol (IP) Address

IP address refers to a unique string of numbers separated by dots (for example, 74.125.224.72) that identifies computers within a network. It is also used to determine the geographic location of computers connected to the network.

Internet Service Provider (ISP)
This is a company that provides Internet access to your computer, mobile phone and other devices.

Interstitial Banners

These are advertisement banners shown between pages on a website. When you click from one page to another, they are shown before the next page is displayed.

JavaScript

This refers to a script language that is written in the code that makes web pages interactive.

Junk Fax

This is a marketing strategy that involves sending unsolicited advertisements through a facsimile transmission.

Junk Mail

Junk mail, also called spam, is an uninvited mail sent out usually by direct marketing or direct mail firms mainly for the purpose of introducing new products, services, merchandise catalogs, investment opportunities, etc.

Keywords

These are words or phrases that are used to trigger search results or describe content. They are used as search terms for search engines and as words that identify the content of a website. For example, the keyword "inspirational calendar" might be used for a calendar offered for sale on a website or in advertisements for audiences using search engines to find calendars. Keywords that contain two or more words are called keyword phrases.

Keyword Ranking

Keyword Ranking means where your website is specifically positioned with a certain keyword on a search engine results page. If your keyword is, for instance, 'whole wheat flour' it can come first, fifth or last on the first search engine result page or appear only on subsequent pages of the results. The box on the next pages shows the first page search results for a query on *'Whole Wheat flour'* (made with Firefox browser) from the Google's 165,000,000 results displayed on June 22, 2020 at 7.48am.

Box 1: First page search results for a query on *Whole Wheat flour*

1.The Difference Between Whole Wheat and White Flour May ...
spoonuniversity.com › Lifestyle
It is common knowledge that *flour* is made up of ground up *wheat grains*. *Wheat* has three parts to it—the bran which is packed with fiber, the endosperm—the ...

2.Whole-wheat flour - Wikipedia
en.wikipedia.org › wiki › Whole-wheat flour
Whole-wheat flour (in the US) or wholemeal flour (in the UK) is a powdery substance, a basic food ingredient, derived by grinding or mashing the whole grain of ...

3. Wheat flour - Wikipedia
en.wikipedia.org › wiki › Wheat flour

White *flour* is made from the endosperm only. Brown *flour* includes some of the grain's germ and bran, while *whole grain* or wholemeal *flour* is   made   from   the   entire ...

4.How To Make Whole Wheat Flour - Tried and Tasty

Apr 9, 2015 - Did you know that making your own *whole wheat flour* is almost easier than buying it? It's fresh, cheaper than store bought, and it's amazing to ...
Rating: 5 - 3 votes - 5 mins - 197 cal

5.King Arthur Premium 100% Whole Wheat Flour - 5 lb. | Shop ...
shop.kingarthurflour.com › items › king-arthur-premiu...

With all the nutritional benefits of whole grains, this flour — America's top-selling *whole wheat flour* — is a pantry all-star: dark in color, rich in flavor, and healthy to ...
Rating: 4.7 - 97 reviews - US$5.95 - In stock

6.Whole Wheat Flour | Baking Ingredients | BAKERpedia
bakerpedia.com › ingredients › whole-wheat-flour

Whole wheat flour is a powder made from grinding the entire kernel. The bran and germ are removed during milling, while the endosperm is finely ground.

7.Is Whole Wheat Lower in Calories Than White

Flour?
www.thespruceeats.com › ... › Ingredient Glossary

When it comes to eating well and cooking healthy meals, *whole wheat flour* is often favored over white flour. Cup for cup, both *whole wheat flour*, and white flour ...

8.A Guide to Different Types of Wheat Flour - The Spruce Eats
www.thespruceeats.com › ... › Cooking FAQs

Feb 12, 2020 - Wheat flour is the most common flour used in baking. These are the differences between ... Pastry Flour. Self-Rising Flour. *Whole Wheat Flour*.

Keyword Stuffing

This is a Search Engine Optimization technique in which a large number of keywords are loaded onto a web page to artificially increase ranking of the page in search results with the goal of getting more traffic to the page. Keyword Stuffing is a web spam, it is, therefore, considered unethical. Some search engines can detect and deal with this despite being hidden away from casual website visitors.

Landing Page

This is the first web page that a visitor "lands on" during a visit to your site. It is the page that displays after clicking on a link. It is also called a 'Lead Capture Page' or 'Destination page' that appears in response to clicking on the search result. This page is usually the response to the "call-to-action" requesting visitors to buy products or subscribe to a service.

Laser Targeted Marketing

This is marketing technique in which online merchants collect consumer data to ensure they target the right people for their products. It lowers the cost of getting customers and allows online merchants to remain alert and responsive to customers' preferences and demand. The data being collected can be customers' age groups, sex and addresses.

Lead

This is a term used to describe a prospective consumer or organization that shows interest in your product or service. It could be someone who has filled out an online form, subscribed to a newsletter, or shared their contact information in exchange for a coupon. Businesses obtain leads through advertising, trade shows, direct mailings, etc.

Lead Magnet

A lead magnet, also known as a content upgrade, is a bonus content given to people usually in exchange for their email address. Examples of lead magnet are a free downloadable e-book and a free video clip.

Lead Nurturing

This is the practice of developing a series of online communications, such as emails and social media messages, to keep your leads engaged as you gradually induce them to make purchases. Leads are sent newsletters, content and promotional materials that keep them engaged. Email marketing is a common form of lead nurturing used to provide prospective buyers with information they need during their buying journey.

Learning Management System (LMS)

This is a software application used to manage online educational courses. LMS enables you to easily create and manage online educational programs without having programming knowledge.

Lifetime Value (LVT)

This is the amount of money a business is expecting to make from an average customer during his/ her entire time with the business as customer.

Link Building

This is the practice of getting web pages from other websites to link to a page on your website to increase the rankings of your website in organic search results.

Listing Fee

This is also called 'insertion fee.' It is an amount of money that online auction or trading sites charge the sellers for listing their products online.

Logistics

Logistics refers to the management of goods, services and resources from their point of origin to the point of consumption to meet the requirements of customers. The resources to be managed include physical items such as food, materials, animals and equipment as well as intangible items like time and information.

Long Tail

This term is used to describe the practice where large volumes of products are sold to few customers instead of selling small volumes of the products to many people. The purpose of doing this is to attract significant amount of traffic by adding up the volume of the products.

Long-Tail Keyword

This is a keyword phrase that typically contains three or more words used to target niche demographics than mass audiences. It is more specific than more commonly searched keywords. Long tail keywords get less search traffic but will usually have a higher conversion value and are often less competitive than generic keywords.

Made to Assemble

This is a form of manufacturing where a factory only produces the essential parts needed for the users to assemble the finished product themselves. This is best for companies wanting to fulfill customer orders quickly.

Made to Order

This is when manufacturing of products takes place only when a specific order is made by customers. In this manufacturing model, handling of inventory is very easy but customers have to wait before products are created. The print-on-demand publishing of books and calendars by www.lulu.com is an example of this form of manufacturing.

Made to Stock

In this kind of manufacturing, the manufacturer creates products in advance based on prediction of customer demand and displays them in showrooms or on shelves.

Map Advertisement

A map advertisement is an advertising placed within the online mapping solutions available like the Google Maps.

Marketing Automation

This is the process of automating marketing tasks, such as emails, marketing campaigns and social media posts instead of doing them manually. With the help of personal information collected from website visitors and existing customers, you can use marketing automation software to send welcome emails, reminders and 'thank you' notes and other customized messages to visitors and customers.

Meme

A meme is a funny picture that comes with a humorous caption often used across social media sites.

Mention

Mention usually refers to "social mentions" which is a direct reference to a username on social media platforms.

Menu

This is a series of links used to help visitors navigate from one web page to another. The menu is often displayed at the top, side, or bottom of the web page.

Merchant Account

This is bank account that allows businesses to accept and process payments through debit or credit cards. It serves as an agreement between a retailer, the merchant bank and payment processor to settle transactions by means of debit or credit cards. If you wish to operate an online business that accepts card payments, you need at least one Internet merchant account.

Microsite

A microsite, which is also called minisite, is a web page or a small cluster of pages that supplements the primary website. It is a specific content site which is designed to exist outside the parent website. Microsites have a specific content used for promotion, a separate URL and less complicated design.

Middle of the Funnel

This term refers to a stage where you publish and distribute content that goes with the needs of customers so as to engage them with your product or brand. The middle of the funnel strategies include email marketing, marketing automation, etc.

Mobile Commerce (mCommerce)

This refers to the use of wireless handheld devices such as mobile phones, smart phones, tablets or personal digital assistants (PDAs) for buying and selling of goods and services online.

Mobile Marketing

Mobile Marketing (also called as Wireless Marketing) is a form of marketing where mobile technology is used to promote personalized goods or services by means of mobile devices such as smart phones, tablets or personal digital assistants (PDAs).

Mobile Optimization

This is the act of ensuring that visitors accessing your website through mobile devices have an impressive user experience practically and visually by optimizing the website content to enable them do what they would like to do on their mobile devices.

Mobile Payments

This is the use of a mobile phone by customers to pay for a variety of goods and services, with the charges assigned to their phone bills. This method replaces or supplements the use of checks, credit cards and other payment methods.

Multi-Channel Ecommerce

This refers to the process of selling goods and services across multiple different channels and devices, including online and on mobile phones.

Native Advertising

This is an online advertising where content is created for paid promotion of a brand on media site in form of an editorial content. The content does not use traditional advertisement formats like banner ads, but includes editorial content such as blogs with the goal of positioning a brand image in the consumer's mind and motivating consumers to take a desired action.

Navigation

Navigation refers to the act of moving through different parts of a website or application. It also refers to the links and other design elements on a web page that allow you move through other parts of the website.

Net Promoter Score (NPS)

This is a metric that measures the willingness of customers to recommend company's products or services to others. With NPS, you can know customer loyalty for a company's brand, products or services. For example, you ask a customer who bought your product this question: "would you recommend this product to your friends?" The response can indicate the customer's willingness to promote the product, criticize it or be indifferent.

News Feed

News Feed (also called as Web Feed) is providing users with frequent transmission of data consisting of news updates. They are given in XML format as summaries or links of updates and on social networking site as a list of updates on your own home page. There are different news feed formats such as RSS and ATOM.

Niche

These are goods or services tailored towards a specialized industry, or a selected product or service.

Niching

This means sticking to a certain theme, product or general idea instead of spreading your business over many different products or categories.

Online Business

This is also called e-business, e-commerce or Internet based business. It is a business where producers or sellers of goods and services transact business with buyers when connected to the Internet.

Off-Page Optimization

This is also called off-page SEO and refers to the ways that can be followed to improve the ranking of a website through promotional means outside the content of the website itself. Off-page SEO can be done through link building, for instance, by means of guest posts so that the articles you post on other websites contain links leading to your own webpage. Other off-page optimization techniques include placement of keywords/website name/webpage in the anchor text of links created; creation of links on authoritative websites and on social media networks; etc.

On-Page Optimization

This is also known as on-page SEO (search engine optimization). It stands for all measures that can be taken within a website to improve its position in search rankings. These measures include updating the page title and description with relevant keywords; adding targeted keywords in all tags, descriptions, and content; and adding alt attributes (alt text) and descriptions to images and videos.

Omni-channel Management

Omni-channel management means providing customers with a seamless shopping experience by ensuring that whether they come to your store offline or through your website or a mobile app or the website, they get the same shopping experience.

Open Rate

This is a percentage representation of the number of people on your email list that opened or viewed a particular email campaign you have undertaken. This percentage is computed by dividing the number of email messages viewed by the total number of email messages sent.

Optin

This is a place where website visitors enter in their details or give you permission to contact them.   It is the form you use to collect information (sign up form) from visitors.

Optin Form

An opt-in form is an online form used for visitors to sign up for your email list or service.

Optin Rate

This refers to the ratio of people who sign up for your email list divided by the total number of visitors on your website. If you get an opt-in rate of 13%, it means that 13 out of every 100 visitors have been signing up for your email list.

Organic Traffic

This term refers to the visitors that land on your website through unpaid results in a search engine.   Organic traffic is obtained when a visitor discovers your web pages through an online search query and clicks on the unpaid search result.

Outsourcing

This is the practice of hiring third party providers to carry out certain functions of your business on your behalf.

Page Rank (PR)

Page rank measures where a page is ranking with a search engine. Highly ranked pages are closer to the number one position on search result pages. (See *keyword ranking* and box 1 related to it).

Pageview

This is the number of times a web page is viewed. When a visitor views the homepage of your website and later moves to another page on your website and hits the back button, it means there are two pageviews.

Parked Domain

This is a domain that is associated with your cPanel account but doesn't have its own content but it is pointed to your primary domain. So, when users try to access your parked domain, they will see the content of your primary or main domain.

Partial Shipment

Partial Shipment, also called Part Shipment, is where the delivery of a shipment takes place in more than one consignment with the permission of the buyer upon which he/she is provided with various codes for order tracking.

Pay Per Action (PPA)

This is a pricing model in which advertisers only pay for a completed action such as, a confirmed sale or email subscription.

Pay Per Click (PPC)

This is also called Cost Per Click (CPC). It is a pricing model in which advertisers pay a fixed amount for every click on their advertisement.

Payment Gateway

This is a merchant service that allows a merchant to accept credit card and other forms of electronic payments with the help of software that facilitates payment transaction by transferring information to Acquiring Banks and transmits responses from Issuing Banks. Payment gateways protect sensitive information by encrypting the data they transmit to merchants and payment processors. Examples of payment gateways include PayPal, Stripe, Paystack and Square.

Payment Service Provider (PSP)

This is a third party that partners with Acquiring Banks to offer merchants the capability to accept and facilitate electronic payments by using various payment methods such as, credit card, debit card, bank transfer, and real-time bank transfer.

Permalink

Permalink, or permanent link, is the URL used to refer to a particular webpage, article, or blog post. It is a link that remains the same for a long period of time.

Plugin

This is a software add-on that you can install onto a program to add functionality or features to it. For example, the Google Chrome browser allows users to install plugins into the browser to add features that are not available in the browser when installed.

Podcasting

A podcast is a digital radio (or video) program downloadable from the Internet. Podcasts are often recorded and edited using home equipment. There is also specialized podcasting software available like Apple's Garage Band or QuickTime Pro for simple recording, mixing, and formatting of the audio files correctly. With podcasts, you can provide content to your target markets.

Point-of-Sale (POS)

Point-Of-Sale is also called Point of Purchase (POP). It is a computerized replacement for a cash register that records and tracks customer orders, processes credit and debit cards.

Pop-Up

A pop-up, also called lightbox, pop-over, or interstitial, is an overlay box that appears in front of a web page. It is often used to invite visitors to your web page to join an email list.

Pop-Ups Pop-Unders

These are advertisements that pop up, or under a web page you are viewing. They open in a new, smaller window.

Profit Margins

A Profit margin is a percentage of selling price turned into profit. It is calculated with the following formula: Profit Margin = (Total Sales – Total Expenses) / Total Sales x 100. You can use profit margin to compare companies in the same industry or between industries to determine which ones are the most profitable.

Qualified Lead

This is a visitor to your website who has opted in to receive communication from it, is aware about your products or service, and wants to learn more. This kind of lead is very likely to turn into a customer.

Quality Score

This refers to the grading system used by Google to determine the relevance of an advertisement to a searcher in certain circumstances, such as showing it in the sponsored space of the search results, and as a result, how much the advertiser should pay for each click.

Query

A query is the word or phrase entered by a user into search engines. If you are looking for a book on poetry written in 2020 and entered "poetry book published in 2020" in Yahoo search engine, this phrase is your search query.

Quick Response Code (QR Code)

This term refers to a machine-readable two-dimensional barcode consisting of an array of black and white squares and often used for storing URLs for easy access to information through smart phones.

Reach

This term refers to the total number of people exposed to a particular marketing campaign.

Really Simple Syndication (RSS)

This is a standard way for people to receive website content through a feed. For example, with an RSS feed reader, a user looking for latest news on international politics from several different websites, can receive and view it in a single feed instead of visiting each website.

Recurring Transaction

A transaction in which a customer authorizes a merchant to charge for goods/services on a prearranged schedule is known as recurring transaction. Recurring transactions take effect where purchases are repeatedly and regularly made. These types of transaction are often used in paying utility bills and magazine subscriptions.

Referral

A referral is when an existing customer invites his / her friends and family members to try a particular product or service.

Referral Traffic

This refers to site visitors that come from direct links on other websites. You get referral traffic especially when other websites post a link recommending your product or service.

Remarketing

Remarketing, also known as retargeting, is a form of online advertising that enables a website to show targeted advertisements repeatedly to visitors when they browse different websites. For example, when you visit a website of a particular product, you also see the advertisement of this website when you browse other websites.

Render

This is the process of generating a visual representation of specific content. Different devices like laptops and smart phones "render" the same content, such as an email or a web page very differently because of their different sizes.

Reseller Hosting

Reseller Hosting is a type of web hosting that allows you (the reseller) to purchase a hosting provider's resources wholesale and resell them to your clients for a profit. Reseller Hosting allows you to create your own branded hosting service and your own pricing structure.

Responsive Design

This is an approach to web design technology that allows a website to adapt automatically to the different devices (laptop, smart phone, tablet, etc.) used by viewers by displaying contents correctly and providing increased usability and complete satisfaction to users.

Response Rate

This refers to the ratio of people who responded to a piece of content divided by the total number of people who received the material. For example, your response rate for an invitation you sent to 200 people is 40% if 80 people responded.

Return on Investment (ROI)

ROI measures the gain or loss generated on an investment relative to its cost. It is usually expressed as a percentage. The Return on Investment formula is: ROI = (Net Profit / Cost of Investment) x 100

Root Domain

The root domain is the highest level within the hierarchy of a site. For example, obmentors.com is a root domain while blog.obmentors.com is a sub-domain.

Screenshot

A screenshot, also called a "screen capture", is an image or snapshot of the computer or mobile device screen.

Search Engine

A search engine is a service that allows users to find relevant content by using a query to search an index of web content. Examples of engines include Google, Yahoo, and Bing.

Search Engine Marketing (SEM)

This is an Internet marketing process involving the purchase of advertisements that appear on search engine result pages (SERPs). When advertisers bid on certain keywords that search engine users usually enter when doing an online query, their advertisements are shown along with the results for the search queries.

Search Engine Optimization (SEO)

This is the practice of improving a website's visibility in search engines in order to increase organic traffic.

Search Engine Results Page (SERP)

This is the page displayed after an online query has been entered on a search engine.

Server

A server is the storage facility for all the files that make up a website.

Service Level Agreement (SLA)

It is a contract signed between the service provider and the customer that documents the services expected from the provider and clearly specifies the performance standards. It can include the nature, quality and scope of the service, responsibilities, expectations and remedies when the requirements are not met by the provider, etc. You need to take time to understand the SLA and what it means to you, your business and your customer.

Session

This is also known as a visit. It refers to any activity engaged in by website visitors on a website, from the time they land on a page to the moment they leave. These activities include downloading a file, clicking on a link, etc.

Sitemap

This is a file that lists all the pages on a website, usually organized hierarchically. With a sitemap on your website it becomes easier for search engine spiders (also called bots or crawlers) to discover all the pages on your website.

Simple Mail Transfer Protocol (SMTP)

This is the method used to move email messages from the sender to the recipient. The SMTP server handles and distributes your email message to one or more recipients.

Shipping

This refers to the physical moving of goods from one point to another. Shipping can take several forms depending on the distance covered and the speed of delivery necessary.

Forms of shipping include ground shipping, air freight shipping and ocean shipping.

Shopping Cart

This is the contents of what a user has added to his online order. All the products appear as a mass order on the page or "in the cart."

Smarketing

This term refers to the process in which sales and marketing teams are made to have a common integrated approach towards achieving business goals. This is done by creating frequent and direct communication between the teams.

Social Media

Social media are media that are designed to be shared. Sharing means allowing users of contents to easily comment on them and send them to other users and at low cost. Examples of social media are Facebook, Twitter, Google Plus, Instagram, Pinterest, Snapchat and Linkedin. Social media also involve blogging, discussion forums and other forms of interactive appearance by which individuals engage in conversations over particular blog posts or events.

Social Media Marketing (SMM)

This refers to marketing efforts done through social media channels.

Social Proof

A **s**ocial proof is the way people's perception of a product or service is influenced by the magnitude and quality of its following. It can be established through testimonials, reviews and trust seals that generate great interest, increase credibility and drive more conversions. There are different types of social proof which include expert social proof, celebrity social proof, wisdom of friends, wisdom of the crowd and user social proof.

Social Signals

These are communicative signals of social media activity, such as shares, votes, pins or likes on social media sites which search engines consider in their ranking algorithms. The signals directly or indirectly provide information through social interactions, emotions, behavior and social relationships on social media sites like Facebook and Pinterest.

Social Traffic

This is the amount of traffic received by a website from various social media channels, such as Linkedin, Twitter and Snapchat. An example of social traffic is when a Linkedin user clicks on a link you shared on your post on Linkedin and clicks the link leading to your website.

Software as a Service (SaaS)

This is a business model for licensing software applications. SaaS is accessed online and is normally subscription-based. SaaS applications are also called as Web-based software, On-demand software or Hosted software. Examples of SaaS include Office 365, Dropbox, and Google Apps.

Spam

This is any message that the recipient did not want or ask for. Examples of spams include emails offering unsolicited products or services as well as false messages claiming that you have won a lottery. Most of these emails automatically go to the Spam folder of your email box.

Spider

Also known as bot or crawler, it refers to software used by search engines to locate and index websites by exploring the Internet. It is used to explore website content, capture information and take it to the database of a search engine for inclusion.

Split Testing (or A/B Test)

This refers to the testing of two separate elements of your ecommerce mix to determine the one that performs better. It is done by splitting a group of people into two or more groups and exposing them to different versions of a webpage, email, advertisements, etc., to determine which one is more effective in motivating people to perform a specific action like buying a product, or submitting emails.

Secure Sockets Layer (SSL)

This is an encryption technology that creates a safe connection between a web server storing all the files that make up a website and the visitors' web browser like Google Chrome or Firefox. With SSL, private information can be transmitted without the risk of eavesdropping, data tampering and message forgery. A website that is protected by SSL starts with "https" instead of "http".

Subdomain

This is a subdivision of a root domain used to cover different languages, regions, or content. If, for example your domain name is <u>obmentors.com</u>, your subdomain could be <u>ar.obmentors.com</u> (content for Arabic language) or <u>blog.obmentors.com</u> (covers content for your blog on the same website).

Terms of Service (TOS)

This is a statement of the commitments of the provider of website service provider to you as well as your rights and responsibilities when using the services. The terms usually cover definition of terms used in writing the terms, privacy policy, ownership of copyright, indemnification, etc. It is advisable for a user of web based services to carefully read the TOS.

Time Lag

In eCommerce, time lag refers to the number of days in between visits before a multi-channel conversion is completed by the visitor. It determines the time between the first interaction date and conversion date.

Timestamp

Timestamp refers to the date and time attached to an event, such as the making social media post.

Title Tag

This term refers to an HTML tag noting the placement of the title of a webpage. The content of the title tag is displayed in search results and in preview when a link to a page is shared through social media channels. It is also seen on the tab of your web browser.

Traffic

In online business, traffic refers to the number of visits received by a web page or website.

Turnkey

This is software or a packaged product that is built, installed and supplied by the manufacturer in its complete, ready to use form.

Third Party Payment Processor

This is a company that handles merchant account payments from various channels such as credit or debit cards for merchant acquiring banks. An example for this is PayPal that lets you accept online payments without a merchant account of your own.

Top of the Funnel

This is the very first stage of the buying process. It is any touch-point that begins an interaction of a customer with your company.

Unique User

This is an individual that visited a website for a given period of time or received specific web content like emails or newsletters. Unique user is counted as a single visitor irrespective of the number of times he or she revisits the site. In Internet marketing, unique users are tracked to determine how many people see web content within a given period of time.

Unique Visitor (UV)

This is a metric for unique individuals that visit a website. Unique visitors are tied to the individual performing the visit. For example, if 5 persons visit a web page 5 times each in a week, the total UVs for the week is 5 while the total number of visits is 25.

Unsubscribe

To unsubscribe means to cancel a service or to remove oneself from a mailing list. In email marketing, an unsubscribe link allows you to stop receiving further emails from the business.

Unsubscribe Rate

This refers to the percentage of email subscribers that have chosen to click the unsubscribe link in relation to the total number of subscribers who received the email. A high unsubscribe rate can be an indication of email spam.

Upsell

This is a sales strategy by which you try to influence a customer into buying something with a higher price, to add on to their purchase, or upgrade their item for the purpose of increasing your revenue. If a customer wants to subscribe for a service at $200 per annum, you can upsell the service by offering it to the buyer at $350 for 2 years. For the buyer, this offer is cheaper because of the $50 discount, for you, it will yield higher revenue. Upselling also includes selling better features or specifications of the selected product, an upgrade or any add-ons.

Uniform Resource Locator (URL)

This is the link that takes a prospective user of website to its specific web page. An example of a URL is https://www.obmentors.com/homepage

Usability

This refers to the ease and efficiency with which your customers can use and interact with your website through the use of computers, mobile and tablet devices bearing in mind the quality of their experience and your conversion rate.

User

The term refers to any person who uses a computer, mobile device, network service and a website.

User Generated Content (UGC)

This is any content created by users on a website by making comments on posts, creating a forum, uploading a video, submitting a blog post, etc.

User Experience (UX)

This is the experience of a customer with a particular business, from the time of being aware of its product or service to the time of using the product or service. Questions meant to find out user experience include: is the product useful? Can you operate it or use it easily? Is it trustworthy?

Viral Content

This is a media content video that spreads quickly through website links and social sharing channels. It is an online content that users would like to share with people so it has a lot of views, reads and clicks.

Visit

A visit, also known as a session, refers to any activity a site visitor undertakes on a website. Examples of these activities include signing up for a service or newsletter, downloading a file and clicking on a link on the same website.

Visitor

A visitor is an individual who visits a website.

Voided

This is credit or debit transaction that is cancelled by the seller, or merchant, after authorization but before completion and settlement.

Wallet

Also known as eWallet, this term refers to software application that facilitates electronic payments using a computer or smart phone for online transactions as well as purchases at physical stores.

Web Analytics

Web analytics, also called Digital Analytics, is a set of strategic methodologies for studying the impact of a website on its users. Web analytics software is used to measure number of visits, unique visitors' count, their online session time, etc.

Web Hosting

This the service offered by companies that store websites and provide Internet connectivity to enable users to have access to contents.

Webcasting

This is a live or on-demand media presentation presented over the Internet. *It* is the process of video broadcasting live over the internet. It operates in real-time and allows for active conversations among and between webcasters and their viewers.

Webinar

A webinar is a type of webcast. It a webinar is an online seminar or web conference done over the Internet in real-time.

Web conferencing

This refers to various types of online collaborative services including web seminars (webinars), webcats and peer-level web meetings.

Web Portal

This term refers to a specially designed website that brings information from diverse sources, like emails, search engines, online forums, etc., in uniform way. It is a web-based platform that gives employees, suppliers, customers and other visitors with a single access point to information. It can be used to provide users with personalized information, such as employee training, customer profile or to enhance the collaboration of information and improve the way users interact with your business.

WhoisGuard

This is a privacy protection service which domain registrars provide to protect your private information from being mined and used for other purposes, such as identity theft or unsolicited marketing. When you buy a domain name the Internet Corporation for Assigned Names and Numbers (ICANN) requires registrars of the domain name to provide them with your contact information which is then added to the Whois database that lists the owners of every domain name online. The database can be searched by anyone on the Internet. The WhoisGuard replaces this personal information with generic WhoisGuard contact information.

WYSIWYG

WYSIWYG is an acronym for "What You See Is What You Get". It is a facility that allows a user editing text and graphic on website to see how the finished work would look like as the user edits them.

XML

XML is a file extension for an Extensible Markup Language (XML) file format. It is a markup language that defines a set of rules for encoding documents in a format that is readable by both human beings and machines. It is used to create common information formats and share both the format and the data on the Internet, intranets, and elsewhere.

XML Sitemap

A sitemap is a way of organizing a website, identifying the URLs and the data under each section. An XML sitemap lists the important pages of your website, making it easy for search engines to find and crawl them all, also helping them understand the structure of your website.

Yield

Yield means the earnings generated and realized on an investment over a particular period of time.

Yuppie

Yuppie is a slang term representing the market segment of young urban professionals. Yuppies are often neat and smart in appearance and like to show off their success by their possessions.

ZCash

ZCash is a cryptocurrency with a decentralized blockchain that provides anonymity for its users and their transactions. ZCash is similar to Bitcoin in many of ways including the open-source o feature, but they differ in the level of privacy they provide, and the ability of being interchanged with other goods or assets of the same type.

Zombies

These are companies that earn just enough money to continue operating and service debt but are unable to pay off their debt.

9 798657 353099